Life of Fred

Apples

Life of Fred

Apples

Stanley F. Schmidt, Ph.D.

Polka Dot Publishing

ISBN: 978-0-9791072-4-5

Library of Congress Catalog Number: 2010936176
Printed and bound in the United States of America

Polka Dot Publishing   Reno, Nevada

To order copies of books in the Life of Fred series,

visit our website PolkaDotPublishing.com

Questions or comments? Email Polka Dot Publishing at lifeoffred@yahoo.com

Second printing

Life of Fred: Apples was illustrated by the author with additional clip art furnished under license from Nova Development Corporation, which holds the copyright to that art.

for Goodness' sake

or as J.S. Bach—who was
never noted for his plain
English—often expressed it:

Ad Majorem Dei Gloriam
(to the greater glory of God)

If you happen to spot an error that the author, the publisher, and the printer missed, please let us know with an email to: lifeoffred@yahoo.com

As a reward, we'll email back to you a list of all the corrections that readers have reported.

A Note Before We Begin

How quickly the days of childhood pass. One moment, they are a little bundle on the bed.

The next moment, they have discovered the delights of triple integrals (as we find the weight of one of Aunt Dorothenia's raisin-and-apple muffins on page 310 in *Life of Fred: Calculus*.)

Fred (and I) would like to be a part of that journey with you. And we would like to do our best to make those years as joyful as they can be. So often mathematics seems to be the most terrifying and tear-filled subject in the curriculum.

It does not have to be.

Math need not be a terrifying experience.

One mom emailed me that she had to set a time limit on how long her child was spending with Fred. Her daughter would start the day with Fred's adventures and not want to study the other subjects.

Pages and pages of worksheets.

(Circle) the three alligators. Underline the two hippos.

Drill-and-kill.

No motivation.

When I taught at the high school and college levels, the most frequent question that other math teachers and I got was, "Why are we studying this stuff?"

The traditional approach in, say, algebra is to show the students how to factor $x^2 + 7x + 12$[*] into $(x + 3)(x + 4)$. Then they get 40 problems to do for homework.

If they asked, "Why are we learning to factor $x^2 + 7x + 12$?" the usual answer was something like, "So that you can simplify fractions

like $\dfrac{x^2 + 7x + 12}{x + 4}$ [**] which is today's lesson."

. . . and 40 more problems to do for homework.

1. $x^2 + 9x + 14$
2. $x^2 + 6x + 5$
3. $x^2 + 5x + 6$
4. $x^2 + 8x + 7$
5. $x^2 + 20x + 100$
6. $x^2 + 14x + 49$
7. $x^2 + 11x + 18$
8. $x^2 + 9x + 18$
9. $x^2 + 19x + 18$
10. $x^2 + 9x + 20$
11. $x^2 + 10x + 21$
12. etc.
13. etc.
14. etc.

the traditional approach

Few students have the courage to ask, "And why are we learning how to simplify fractions?" They just bow their heads and suffer through it.

Is there any wonder that kids don't seem to remember the math that they "learned"?

---

[*] To factor $x^2 + 7x + 12$, you find two numbers that add to 7 and that multiply to 12. That gives you the answer of $(x + 3)(x + 4)$.

[**] $\dfrac{x^2 + 7x + 12}{x + 4} = \dfrac{(x + 3)(x + 4)}{x + 4} = \dfrac{(x + 3)(\cancel{x + 4})}{\cancel{x + 4}} = x + 3$

In contrast, in the *Life of Fred* series, every piece of mathematics
✓ first happens in Fred's everyday life,
✓ he needs it,
✓ then we do it.

Everything is motivated—everything from introducing the number zero in this book (as the number of elephants that Fred owns) to hyperbolic trigonometric functions, where we find three(!) uses for them on page 250 of *Life of Fred: Calculus* when Fred and the 8'2" lion enter an all-you-can-eat buffet.

Mary Poppins said that a spoonful of sugar isn't a bad thing. We use lots of sugar.

HOW THIS BOOK IS ORGANIZED

Each chapter is about six pages. At the end of each chapter is a Your Turn to Play.

Have a paper and pencil handy before you sit down to read.

Each Your Turn to Play consists of about three or four questions. Have your child write out the answers—not just orally answer them.

After all the questions are answered, then take a peek at my answers that are given on the next page. At this point your child has *earned* the right to go on to the next chapter.

Don't just allow your child to read the questions and look at the answers. Your child won't learn as much taking that shortcut. Put something over the answers if there is a temptation to cheat. Or use

Genuine plastic

clothes pins to prevent premature turning of the page. One reader suggested that I sell plastic Fred Heads to cover the answers.

CALCULATORS?

Not now. There will be plenty of time later (when you hit Pre-Algebra). Right now in arithmetic, our job is to learn the addition and multiplication facts by heart.

Contents

Chapter One
Early in the Morning

Fred lay in his sleeping bag. It was early in the morning, and it was still dark outside. Fred took his flashlight and shined it on the clock on the wall.

It was five o'clock. If this were summertime, it would be getting light by now. But it was February. It would be dark for another couple of hours.

Fred liked to go jogging in the morning, but he knew that if he jogged in the dark he would trip and fall a lot. He was going to wait two more hours until it was seven o'clock before he went out running.

Fred did not sleep in a regular bed like most five-year-olds. He did not own a bed. He slept in a sleeping bag.

Kingie

Five years ago when he came to KITTENS University, he owned nothing except his doll, Kingie.

Fred liked Kingie to sleep right next to him.

KITTENS University gave Fred a room on the third floor of the math building to use as his office. He made it into his home.

The only thing in that room was a big old desk. Fred used to sleep on the top of the desk. When the janitor found out what Fred was doing, the janitor gave him a little sleeping bag. It was only three feet long, but that was just the right size for Fred. He put the sleeping bag under his desk. That made it a safe little cave for Kingie and him.

Fred liked to talk to Kingie. Kingie didn't say very much, but he was a very good listener. Years ago Fred got Kingie as a free toy at the King of French Fries restaurant. When Kingie was new, Fred could squeeze his tummy and he would sing a little song about french fries:

♪ ♪ Butter fries are butter. ♪♪

The song didn't make much sense.

14

About two weeks after Fred got Kingie, his battery died, and he stopped singing. Fred put a new battery in Kingie, but Kingie didn't sing the Butter fries song anymore. But Kingie still liked to listen to whatever Fred had to say.

Fred told Kingie, "Let's wait two hours before we get up. It's five o'clock now, and if we wait until seven o'clock it will be light outside."

Kingie didn't say anything, but Fred knew what Kingie was thinking: 5 + 2 = 7.

Fred opened a desk drawer and took out some pencils.

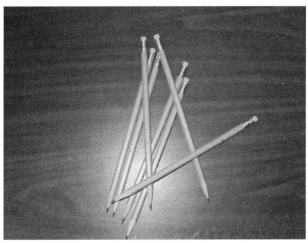

7 pencils

Kingie counted them. There were seven pencils. Fred had a very smart doll.

Then Fred straightened out the pencils.

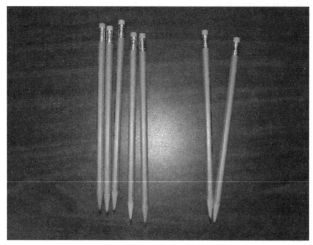

5 + 2 is 7

He asked Kingie, "Now how many pencils are there?" Fred knew that Kingie was giggling since that was such a silly question. If you start with seven pencils and you move them around you will still have seven pencils. Even a doll knows that is true.

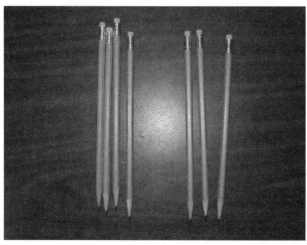

4 + 3 is 7

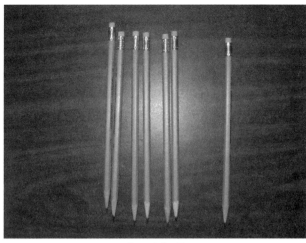

6 + 1 is 7

Please take out a sheet of paper and write your answers. After you are all done, you can check your work on the next page.

Your Turn to Play

1. Sometimes, we write "6 + 1 is 7." Sometimes, we use an equals sign and write "6 + 1 = 7."

How would you write "4 + 3 is 7" using an equals sign?

2. We know that 4 pencils plus 3 pencils equals 7 pencils.

What does 4 trees plus 3 trees equal?

3. We know that 5 + 2 = 7.

What does 2 + 5 equal?

........**ANSWERS**.......

1. 4 + 3 = 7

2. 4 trees plus 3 trees equals 7 trees.

3. 2 + 5 = 7

     If 5 + 2 = 7   then 2 + 5 = 7.

     If 8 + 5 = 13   then 5 + 8 = 13.

     If 10 + 20 = 30   then 20 + 10 = 30.

     x + y always gives the same answer as y + x
where x and y can be any numbers.

Chapter Two
Closer to Sunrise

Fred loved to play with his flashlight. When Fred shined his light on Kingie, he looked like this:

When he didn't shine his light on Kingie, he looked like this:

Fred put his seven pencils back into his desk drawer. He liked to keep his office neat. He would never leave pencils lying on the floor. Some of his students called him, "No Mess Fred."

Time out!

Did you notice that? I wrote, "Some of *his students*. . . ."
Fred has students. Please let me explain.
Fact number one: Fred is five years old.
Fact number two: He is not a student at KITTENS University.

Fact number three: When Fred was very young, he read a lot of books. He especially liked to read books about math.

Fact number four: When Fred was nine months old, he came to KITTENS University to be a math teacher! (The whole story is told in *Life of Fred: Calculus*.)

Kingie took the flashlight and shined it on Fred.

When he turned off the flashlight, Fred looked like this:

When Kingie pointed the flashlight straight at the wall, it made a circle.

When he tipped the flashlight a little bit, it made an ellipse on the wall. (pronounced: e-LIPS)

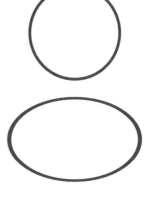

Fred took out a piece of binder paper.   He
wanted to show Kingie how to draw things.   He
knew Kingie wanted him to draw a dog.

Then Kingie wanted Fred to draw a mouse.

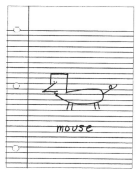

Kingie giggled.   Fred's mouse looked
exactly like Fred's dog. Fred drew the mouse
again.

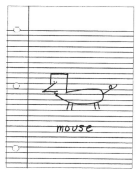

That was much better.

Fred showed Kingie how to draw all kinds
of animals.

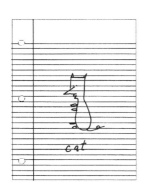 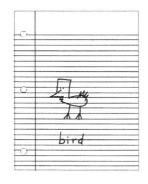 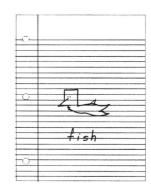

They looked at the clock again.

It was six o'clock. In one hour it would be
seven o'clock and Fred could go jogging. 6 + 1 =
7.

He took all the drawings and put them in a
desk drawer marked: **My Art**. Other teachers
had desks that were messy.
When Fred finished with
something, he put it away.

Kingie thought about the six drawings that Fred had made and wished that he had a piece of paper to make a drawing. This would have been Kingie's drawing:

Art by Kingie

Fred's doll could draw better than Fred could.

Art by Fred

Please take out a sheet of paper and write your answers. After you are all done, you can check your work on the next page.

Your Turn to Play

1. Fred made six drawings. Fred's six drawings plus Kingie's one drawing equals how many drawings?

2. Fill in the blank: 5 + 2 = 7.

3. Fill in the blank: 4 + __ = 7.

. . . . ANSWERS . . . .

1. Fred's six drawings plus Kingie's one drawing equals seven drawings. $6 + 1 = 7$.

2. $5 + 2 = 7$

3. $4 + 3 = 7$

There are seven days in a week.

There are five weekdays: Monday

Tuesday

Wednesday

Thursday

Friday

That leaves two days for the weekend:

Saturday

Sunday

5 weekdays + 2 days on the weekend equals 7 days in a week.

Chapter Three
What to Do before Dawn

Fred looked at the clock again. It was just a little bit after six o'clock. He got up and rolled up his sleeping bag.

He changed out of his pajamas into his jogging clothes. He wondered what to do next.

✓ It wasn't time to brush his teeth because he did that after breakfast.

✓ It wasn't time to go teach his first class because that didn't start until eight o'clock.

✓ It wasn't time to arrange the books on the walls of his office because he always kept them in order.

During the five years that Fred had taught at KITTENS University, he bought books—lots of books. He had arranged his books by their titles.

About the Stars
Accepting Adulthood
Adjust Your Attitude
Algebra for Today's World
. . .

All the way down to

. . .
Whistling for Beginners
Xylophones Are Fun to Play
Zippers in the Middle Ages

Kingie asked Fred to read him a book. Fred pulled *Months of the Year* off the shelf. Since it was February, he turned to the chapter entitled **FEBRUARY**.

Fred read to Kingie: **February is such a silly month. It cannot decide how many days it has. In most years it has 28 days. But once every four years, February decides to have 29 days.**

The years in which February has 29 days are called leap years.

February is Library Lover's Month.

It is National Snack Food Month. This was started by the National Snack Food Association because snack food sales were often slow in February.

February is also Black History Month, American Heart Month, and National Chocolate Lover's Month.

It is also the month that gets spelled wrong most often. After people write January, they want to spell February the way it sounds. The correct way to spell February is FebRUary, not Febuary.

—the end—

Kingie liked it when Fred read to him. He smiled when Fred had finished the chapter.

Kingie asked Fred, "Who gets to say that February is Library Lover's Month?"

"That's easy," Fred answered. "Anybody can say that February is anything they want."

Fred gave Kingie a hug and told him, "I love you every month of the year."

It was almost seven o'clock, and Fred was getting ready to go jogging. He put Kingie on top of his desk.

Kingie had one more question: "If this is February and if this is Kansas, shouldn't you wear warmer clothes?"

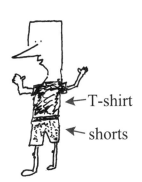

Fred looked out the window from his office on the third floor. He held Kingie up so that he could see too.

It was just getting light. Everything was white. The ground looked white. The houses looked white. The trees looked white.

White! White ground, white houses, white trees—that's snow!

Kingie told Fred to wear boots.

and pants   and mittens   and a scarf

and a coat   and ear muffs   and a hat.

It was seven o'clock. Fred put Kingie back on top of his desk, gave him another hug, and headed out of his office.

Please take out a sheet of paper and write your answers. After you are all done, you can check your work on the next page.

Your Turn to Play

1. February is the most misspelled month. Guess which is the most misspelled day of the week: Sunday, Monday, Tuesday, Wednesday, Thursday, Friday, or Saturday.

2. Sunday is the *first* day of the week. Monday is the *second* day of the week. What day of the week is Saturday?

3. 4 + ? = 7

4. 5 + ? = 7

5. 3 + ? = 7

6. Which animal did Fred draw?

. . . . **ANSWERS** . . . .

1. I think that WeDNESday is the most misspelled. But some other people think that SatURday is also pretty hard to spell. Almost everyone can spell Sunday.

2. Sunday → first day of the week

    Monday → second day of the week

    Tuesday → third day of the week

    Wednesday → fourth day of the week

    Thursday → fifth day of the week

    Friday → sixth day of the week

    Saturday → seventh day of the week

3. 4 + 3 = 7

4. 5 + 2 = 7

5. 3 + 4 = 7

6. Fred was trying to draw a snake. Some people think it looks more like a worm. One person said it looks like a piece of Fred spaghetti.

Chapter Four
Going Jogging at Dawn

Fred closed the door to his office. He walked past the vending machines in the hallway. He ran down the two flights of stairs and out into the cold February morning.

KITTENS University has a school newspaper.

THE KITTEN Caboodle

The Official Campus Newspaper of KITTENS University Monday 6 a.m.   10¢

Big Storm Coming!

KANSAS: The weather is changing today. A dangerous surprise storm is coming. It will bring lots of snow and wind.

The best place to be is inside. Do not go outside unless you really have to.

KITTENS President

Our president has cancelled all classes today because of the bad weather.

Question: Who did not read today's paper?

Answer:

When Fred started jogging, there was only a couple inches of snow on the ground. That was not unusual for Kansas in February.

As he jogged it started to snow harder and harder. And the temperature was falling . . .

$$40°$$
$$35°$$
$$30°$$
$$25°$$
$$20°$$
$$15°$$
$$10°$$
$$5°$$
$$0°$$
$$-5°$$
$$-10°$$
$$-15°$$

It was 15 degrees below zero. That is pretty cold.

And the snow was getting deeper and deeper.

Then the wind picked up speed and blew off
Fred's hat.

Instead of his usual ten-mile jog, he decided
to take a two-mile jog. This shorter jog would
take him by an apple tree on the university
campus. Everyone at the university was
allowed to pick apples from that tree. Fred was
thinking of having an apple for his
breakfast.

The apple tree was on the
north side of campus. Fred had
not been to the north side for a long
time. When he got there, he was in for a
surprise.

Here is what the apple tree looked like:

In the summertime that
tree had lots of apples, but
this was February. It was
not apple time.

Every year when it starts to get cold, apple trees lose all of their leaves and apples. During the wintertime they are resting. When springtime comes, they start putting out new leaves and flowers. Apple trees are deciduous. (pronounced: dee-SID-you-us)

Peach trees are deciduous. Plum trees are deciduous. Apricot trees are deciduous.

Roses are deciduous.

summertime   wintertime

When you are about two years old, you have all 20 of your baby teeth. Ten are on the top, and ten on the bottom. 10 + 10 = 20.

When you are about six or seven years old, you start to lose your baby teeth and get your permanent (adult) teeth.

Since Fred is only five years old, he hasn't started losing his baby teeth yet. Baby teeth are called deciduous teeth.

If Fred's nose were deciduous:

Please take out a sheet of paper and write your answers. After you are all done, you can check your work on the next page.

Your Turn to Play

1. When the temperature was falling, we were counting (backwards) by fives:

    40°
      35°
        30°
          25°
            20° etc.

Let's count (forward) by fives from 0 to 100:

  0, 5, 10, 15, (please fill in the missing numbers), 95, 100.

2. 5 + 2 = ?

3. We know that 10 + 10 = 20.
Can you guess what 10 + 10 + 10 equals?

········**ANSWERS**·······

1. 0, 5, 10, 15, 20, 25, 30, 35, 40, 45, 50, 55, 60, 65, 70, 75, 80, 85, 90, 95, 100.

2. $5 + 2 = 7$

3. $10 + 10 + 10 = 30$

Another one of Fred's drawings:

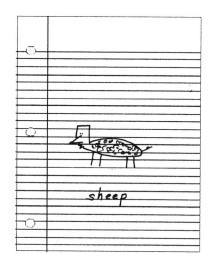

You could tell it was a sheep because of the wool on its body.

Chapter Five
Feeling Cold

It was 15 degrees below zero. It was windy. Fred had lost his hat, and he was starting to feel cold.

The coldest part of Fred was his nose. He  took off one of his mittens and put it on his nose. But that was silly. Now his nose was warm, but his hand was cold.

He got another idea. He put his mitten back on his hand and put his ear muffs on his nose.

This was perfect. His hands were warm. His nose was warm. He didn't need to keep his ears warm, because he doesn't have any ears.

If Fred had ears, he would look funny.

rabbit ears   mouse ears   pointy ears   big ears

Fred knew it was time to get back so that he could teach his first class at eight o'clock. So Fred hurried back to his office in the math building.

The math building was three stories tall. He entered the building on the first floor.

He climbed to the third floor.

Third floor →
Second floor →
First floor →

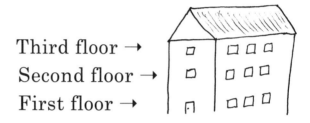

He walked past the vending machines in the hallway and opened his office door. Kingie was waiting for him on top of his desk where Fred had left him.

Fred put his ear muffs and his mittens next to Kingie. He told Kingie, "I have to get ready for my classes."

Kingie already knew that. Every weekday (Monday, Tuesday, Wednesday, Thursday, and Friday) Fred would teach.

Fred wrote up some notes for his algebra class.

Algebra

February

Everyone knows 3 + 4 = 7.

Three ducks plus four ducks equals seven ducks.

This is algebra:

$3x + 4x = 7x$

$3y + 4y = 7y$

$3z + 4z = 7z$

"What are those things?" Kingie asked.

Kingie was pointing to Fred's ducks  and said, "Those ducks are silly. Real ducks don't have noses!"

Fred said, "You are right." Fred took out another piece of paper and drew a duck without a nose.

There was something wrong with Fred's second drawing of a duck, but Kingie wasn't sure what.

Fred's Second Duck

Kingie took Fred's notes and drew in seven ducks.

Algebra

February

Everyone knows 3 + 4 = 7.

Three ducks plus four ducks equals seven ducks.

This is algebra:

$$3x + 4x = 7x$$
$$3y + 4y = 7y$$
$$3z + 4z = 7z$$

Fred was very good at math, but his doll could draw better than he could.

Please take out a sheet of paper and write your answers. After you are all done, you can check your work on the next page.

Your Turn to Play

1. What do 5 ellipses plus 2 ellipses equal?

2. Draw 3 elephants plus 4 elephants. (On the next page you can see Fred's drawings.)

3. Let's do some algebra.

3x + 4x = ?

4. What is the second day of the week?

5. What is the second month of the year?

.......ANSWERS ....

1. 5 ellipses plus 2 ellipses equal 7 ellipses.

2.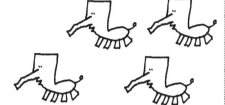

$$3 + 4 = 7$$

3. 3x + 4x = 7x

4. Sunday

    Monday ☞ is the second day of the week.

    Tuesday

    Wednesday

    Thursday

    Friday

    Saturday

5. February is the second month of the year.

Chapter Six
Fred Goes to Class

It was almost eight o'clock. Fred put on his ear muffs and his mittens. He put his lecture notes in his pocket.

He gave Kingie a hug and
headed out the door and
walked past the vending machines and
ran down the two flights of stairs and
headed out into the snow and
jogged across the campus and
arrived at the Archimedes building.

Fred's classroom was in the Archimedes building. (arca-ME-dees)

Archimedes Thoughtful

This is a painting of Archimedes.

It was painted by Fetti 1800 years after Archimedes died.

Fred walked into the classroom and looked at the clock on the wall. It was exactly eight o'clock. He was right on time.

But where were the students? All the chairs were empty. Fred was alone.

He asked himself, "Is it eight o'clock in the morning or is it eight o'clock in the evening?"

It was light outside. It must be 8 a.m. ("a.m." means before noon. In Latin, a.m. stands for *ante meridiem*. *Ante* means "before" and *meridiem* means "noon.")

Fred ran down the hallway to find the janitor. There was no one in the hall, and the janitor's door was locked.

There was a note on the janitor's door.

7 a.m.

As you all know, all classes are cancelled because of the big snow. I'm going home before it gets really bad.

That explains everything, Fred thought to himself. *I wonder what "really bad" means. I already lost my hat in the wind.*

Fred did not have to wait long to find out what "really bad" meant. He heard a big **Ka-Boom!** That was thunder.

He looked out the window and saw the lightning and heard another Ka-Boom.

Fred was delighted. He loved to see the lightning and hear the thunder. For him it was like a great big show. As long as he was inside where it was safe and warm, he was happy.

He got a chair from one of the classrooms and sat down and watched the show. One of the most fun parts was not knowing when the next lightning flash would happen. Sometimes there would be a lot of lightning, and sometimes he would have to wait for a couple of minutes before the next lightning bolt.

He started singing his favorite thunder-and-lightning song. He couldn't remember all the words. He sang:

   ♪♫ **Eight tiny reindeer**

      Donner and Blitzen.   ♫♪

Donner in German means "thunder," and *Blitz* means "lightning." (Blitzen rhymes with Vixen.)

Sometimes Fred would sing **Blitzen and Donner**, because you always see the lightning before you hear the thunder.

Some dogs get frightened by thunder. When they hear the sound, they run and hide under a bed. They don't understand that thunder and lightning can be a lot of fun if you are inside a house. Most dogs can't sing: ♪Donner and Blitzen. ♪♪

Fred sat there watching the show for about an hour until it was nine o'clock.

By then the lightning and thunder had stopped. They were replaced by a heavy rain.

Sometimes when it rains, it is just a light sprinkle. There is barely enough water to make the ground damp.

a three-drop rain

But that was not the case today. This was a big, heavy, wet rain.

a million-drop rain

Your Turn to Play

(Did you remember to take out a piece of paper?)

1. These are a hundred stars.
It is a square with 10 rows and 10 columns.

```
   1  2  3  4  5  6  7  8  9  10
1  ★  ★  ★  ★  ★  ★  ★  ★  ★  ★
2  ★  ★  ★  ★  ★  ★  ★  ★  ★  ★
3  ★  ★  ★  ★  ★  ★  ★  ★  ★  ★
4  ★  ★  ★  ★  ★  ★  ★  ★  ★  ★
5  ★  ★  ★  ★  ★  ★  ★  ★  ★  ★
6  ★  ★  ★  ★  ★  ★  ★  ★  ★  ★
7  ★  ★  ★  ★  ★  ★  ★  ★  ★  ★
8  ★  ★  ★  ★  ★  ★  ★  ★  ★  ★
9  ★  ★  ★  ★  ★  ★  ★  ★  ★  ★
10 ★  ★  ★  ★  ★  ★  ★  ★  ★  ★
```

A hundred of these squares would be ten thousand.
A hundred ten thousands would be a million.
Do you think a million is a big number?

2. 6 drops plus 1 drop equals how many drops?
3. $2x + 5x = ?$
4. How do you spell the third day of the week?

wednesday
wednesday

.......**ANSWERS**.......

1. This is a million: 1,000,000. Most people think that it is a big number.

One day Archimedes decided to figure out how many grains of sand it would take to fill up the whole universe. The number of grains of sand would be one vigintillion. When you get to algebra, we will write a vigintillion as 10^{63}. Since you are not in algebra yet, we have to write one vigintillion as:
1,000,000,000,000,000,000,000,000,000,000,000,
000,000,000,000,000,000,000,000,000. I think that is a big number.

2. 6 drops plus 1 drop equals 7 drops.

3. $2x + 5x = 7x$

4. Sunday
    Monday
    Tuesday ✍ the third day of the week

In order to figure out how many grains of sand it would take to fill up the whole universe, Archimedes first worked out how large the universe is. Then he figured out it would take a vigintillion grains of sand to fill it up.

It took him about eight pages and is called Αρχιμήδης Ψαμμίτης (or in English: *The Sand Reckoner).*

Chapter Seven
Waiting for the Rain to Stop

Fred was all alone in the Archimedes building. The classrooms were empty. The halls were empty. Even the janitor had gone home.

It was a million-drop rain and Fred didn't want to go outside. He decided to play at the blackboard.

He had seen Domenico Fetti's painting of Archimedes. Fetti did his painting in 1620.

 This is how Fetti imagined Archimedes looked. He didn't know for sure since no one ever took a photograph of Archimedes.

Archimedes was born 287 years before Christ (287 BC), and photography was invented over 2,100 years later.

Fred drew on the blackboard what he thought Archimedes looked like. Fetti had named his picture *Archimedes Thoughtful.* Fred named his picture ⟶  *Happy Archimedes*

Archimedes was a good name for the building that had the math classroom in it. If you don't count people who have lived recently (say, in the last 500 years), Archimedes is probably the best mathematician who has ever lived.

He also invented new machines and studied the stars. But he never drew a picture of Fred.

Archimedes was studying a math diagram when a soldier ordered him to get up and follow him. Archimedes answered: μή μοη τούς κήκλους τάραττε. He was speaking in Greek. He said these words in Greek, because he was Greek.

If Archimedes had spoken in Latin, he would have said, "Noli turbare circulos meos."

He had been rude and said, "Don't mess with my circles." Those were the last words he ever said.

Moral:
Don't be rude—
especially to people with swords.

New Moral:
Don't be rude—to anybody!

Fred had been drawing various pictures on the blackboard for an hour.

Archimedes   his dog   his cat

It was now ten o'clock, and the rain had stopped.

Fred looked out the window. The sun was a pale yellow. It wasn't very bright.

The rain and the sun had melted all the snow. That made a lot of water.

A lot of water is called a flood.

When Fred walked outside the Archimedes building, he knew he was in a flood.

Fred knew how to swim, so this was going to be fun. It was like a big swimming pool where he could play as long as he liked.

He lived in Kansas.

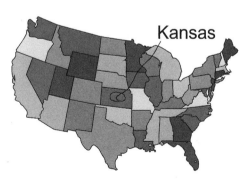

Kansas

He didn't have to worry about alligators.

There are no alligators in Kansas.

He didn't have to worry about a giant whale swallowing him up.

There are no whales in Kansas.

He didn't have to worry about being run over by a big ocean liner.

There are no ocean liners in Kansas.

Your Turn to Play

1. 3 alligators plus 4 alligators equals how many alligators?
2. 4y + 3y = ?
3. How do you spell the fifth day of the week?
4. Name a famous mathematician who lived at least a thousand years ago.

. . . . ANSWERS . . . .

1. 3 alligators plus 4 alligators equals 7 alligators.
(If you wrote that 3 alligators plus 4 alligators equals
7 horses, that would be silly.)

2. $4y + 3y = 7y$

3. Sunday
    Monday
    Tuesday
    Wednesday
    Thursday   ☞ the fifth day of the week

4. There are several famous mathematicians who lived
over a thousand years ago. Archimedes was one of
them. Another possible answer was Euclid (YOU-clid)
who wrote a famous geometry book (*The Elements*).

---

small essay

Where to Live

People live almost everywhere on the earth.
Every place has some nice things you can say
about it.

If you lived near the North Pole, you might
not need air conditioning.

If you lived in Kansas, you wouldn't have to
worry about big ocean liners running you over.

If you lived where you are right now, you
would be close to people who love you.

Chapter Eight
Swimming

Fred swam over to the north side of campus to look at the apple tree. No one needed to water that tree today. Since it was still February, there were still no apples on that tree.

Fred loved swimming. First, he swam around in a big circle.

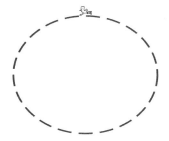

Then he swam around in a big ellipse.

Then in a square.

As the clouds blew away, the sun became brighter and brighter. The temperature was going up.

0° 5° 10° 15° 20° 25° 30° 35° 40° 45°

This is called counting by fives. If you have to count to 100, it is a lot faster to count by fives than to count by ones: 1, 2, 3, 4, 5, 6, 7, 8, 9, 10, 11, 12, 13, 14, and so on.

The water was going down.

Two fish decided to swim over to the lake that is near the campus. If they waited until the flood was gone, then they would have to walk to the lake. Fish are not very good at walking.

Fish can swim but not walk.

Fred can swim and walk.

But fish can do something that Fred can't do. They can breathe underwater.

When Fred draws a picture of a fish, it is a silly picture.

error

Noses are good when you are breathing air, but they are no good underwater.

If you look at a globe of the world, you can see that most of the earth is covered with water. There are lots of oceans.

There are no oceans that touch Kansas,

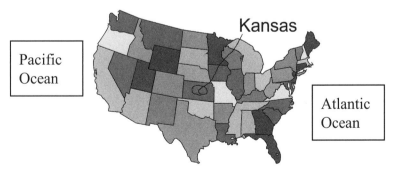

Kansas

Pacific Ocean

Atlantic Ocean

but there are two oceans that touch the United States. Lots of fish live in the oceans, but none of them look like this:

Look! No noses.

whale

These all live in the ocean, but they do not
all breathe water. A whale breathes air. A
whale is not a fish. It comes to the surface,
takes a breath of air, and then dives under the
water to play.

If someone asks you for the name of an
animal that breathes air but cannot walk, you
could say, "a whale."

You could also say that
little babies can breathe air but
cannot walk.

Of course, when I am napping, I am breathing but I cannot walk.

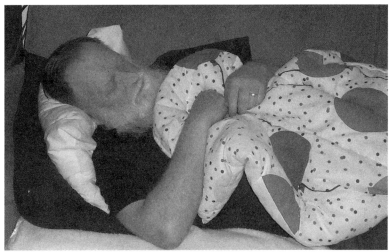

happy Stan

Your Turn to Play

1. Counting by fives, write down the numbers between 35 and 100. It starts: 35, 40, 45. . . .

2. There were five fish in the lake near the campus. Two more fish came over and joined them. How many fish are now in the lake?

3. There are zero whales in Kansas.  How many ocean liners are in Kansas?

4. Which is true?

   A) Archimedes was a famous baseball player.

   B) Archimedes was a whale.

   C) Archimedes was a mathematician.

· · · · · · **ANSWERS** · · · · · ·

1. Counting by fives:
    35, 40, 45, 50, 55, 60, 65, 70, 75, 80, 85, 90, 95, 100.
2. Five fish plus two fish equals seven fish.
    5 + 2 = 7
3. There are zero ocean liners in Kansas.
4. The correct answer is C) Archimedes was a mathematician.

It's fun to play the "There Are Zero . . ." game.

✓ There are zero elephants in my cereal bowl.

✓ There are zero palm trees in my hair.

✓ There are zero birthday cakes floating in my bathtub.

Chapter Nine
To the Lake

The water went down. Fred was standing on dry land. It was still February. It was still not the time for apples.

So Fred decided to walk to the lake near the campus. He wanted to see where the fish had gone.

When he got to the lake he saw the two fish that had been near the apple tree. Those two fish had joined the five fish that were already in the lake.

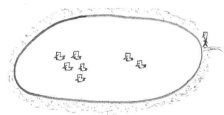

The seven fish looked very happy swimming in the water. 5 + 2 = 7

The lake looked like an ellipse.

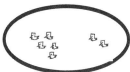

Fred giggled. He thought of how you could make an ellipse. You could start with a circle.

And then you could put an elephant on top of it.

And then the elephant would squish the circle down into an ellipse.

A really big elephant would make a very flat ellipse.

Or, if you wanted an ellipse that looked like this,

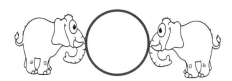

it would take one elephant on each side to push the circle

into an ellipse.

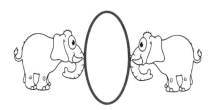

Sometimes Fred could be very silly.

Fred looked out over the lake. He knew there were zero alligators in the lake. There were zero ocean liners in the lake. And there were zero birthday cakes floating on the lake.

Zero is a very handy number.

It's hard to name a set that contains exactly 5 members. The only one I can think of is the set of weekdays: {Monday, Tuesday, Wednesday, Thursday, Friday}.

It is a little easier to think of a set that contains 4 members. {My four grandparents} or the four directions on a compass {north, east, south, west}.

Sets that contain 3 members are even easier to think of. {The 3 states that begin with "O": Ohio, Oklahoma, and Oregon}. {The 3 states that water comes in: solid (ice), liquid, and gas (steam)}. {The 3 floors in Fred's math building that he lives in}.

There are lots of sets with exactly 2 members. {Your left and right hands}. {Your eyes}. {The two oceans that touch the United States: the Pacific Ocean and the Atlantic Ocean}.

Lots of sets contain only one member. {You—there is only one of you}. {Our sun}. {Your nose}. {Your one life}. {God}.

But the most common set is the set that contains zero members.

Let's have a contest! You name a set with one member in it, and I'll name three sets that have no members in it.

YOU	ME
{the sun}	{the sun that is purple} {the sun that weighs one pound} {the sun that likes to dance}
{my nose}	{the nose on the top of your head} {the noses on your elbows} {the nose that likes to dance}
{the dolls that Fred owns: Kingie}	{the elephants that Fred owns} {the mice that Fred owns} {the horses that Fred owns}

Most sets have zero members. I think it is nature's favorite number.

{Months that have only 1 day in them}	zero
{Months that have exactly 2 days in them}	zero
{Months that have exactly 3 days in them}	zero
{Months that have exactly 4 days in them}	zero
{Months that have exactly 5 days in them}	zero

{Months that have exactly 6 days in them}   zero
{Months that have exactly 7 days in them}   zero
{Months that have exactly 8 days in them}   zero
{Months that have exactly 9 days in them}   zero
{Months that have exactly 10 days in them}   zero
{Months that have exactly 11 days in them}   zero
{Months that have exactly 12 days in them}   zero
{Months that have exactly 13 days in them}   zero
{Months that have exactly 14 days in them}   zero
{Months that have exactly 15 days in them}   zero
{Months that have exactly 16 days in them}   zero
{Months that have exactly 17 days in them}   zero
{Months that have exactly 18 days in them}   zero
{Months that have exactly 19 days in them}   zero
{Months that have exactly 20 days in them}   zero
{Months that have exactly 21 days in them}   zero
{Months that have exactly 22 days in them}   zero
{Months that have exactly 23 days in them}   zero
{Months that have exactly 24 days in them}   zero
{Months that have exactly 25 days in them}   zero
{Months that have exactly 26 days in them}   zero
{Months that have exactly 27 days in them}   zero
{Months that have exactly 28 or 29 days in them}   one
{Months that have exactly 30 days in them}   four
{Months that have exactly 31 days in them}   seven
{Months that have exactly 32 days in them}   zero
{Months that have exactly 33 days in them}   zero
{Months that have exactly 34 days in them}   zero
{Months that have exactly 35 days in them}   zero
{Months that have exactly 36 days in them}   zero
{Months that have exactly 37 days in them}   zero
{Months that have exactly 38 days in them}   zero
{Months that have exactly 39 days in them}   zero

And this list could go on forever. And only 3 sets out of the millions of sets have more than zero members. Zero is really popular.

Your Turn to Play

1. I can name a set with 17 members. That is not hard to do. It is the set of all numbers from 1 to 17: {1, 2, 3, 4, 5, 6, 7, 8, 9, 10, 11, 12, 13, 14, 15, 16, 17}. If you don't believe me, you can count them.

   Name a set with 500 members in it.

2. If you put an elephant on top of this ellipse and squished it until it was round, what shape would it become?

3. Counting by fives, write down the numbers between 20 and 45.

4. It is an hour since it stopped raining. What time is it now?

5. What is the third day of the week?

6. What is the third month of the year?

7. What is the first thing you think of when you hear "ice cream"?

8. 3 + 4 = ?

. . . . ANSWERS . . . .

1. One possibility is the set of all numbers from 1 to 500. (Another possibility is the set of all numbers from 2 to 501. Another possibility is the sheets in a ream of paper. Paper is often packaged in reams, which are 500 sheets.)

2. An ellipse that is squished until it is round becomes a circle.

3. 20, 25, 30, 35, 40, 45

4. It is eleven o'clock. (Or you could have written 11 o'clock or 11:00 a.m.)

5. Sunday

   Monday

   Tuesday   ✒ the third day of the week

6.   January

     February

     March   ✒ the third month of the year

7. Your answer may be different than mine. My first thought was, "Where?" Yours might have been, "Cold," or "Delicious," or "Chocolate," or "Two scoops," or "Birthday party."

8. $3 + 4 = 7$

One fun thing to play in the car with your parents is for you to name a set with one member in it, and have them name a set with three members in it. Repeat until someone can't think of any. I bet you will win.

Chapter Ten
Getting a Boat

O n the shore of the lake, Fred found a set of sailboats.

4   3

Four of them were on the left of the boathouse, and three of them were on the right.

Fred thought to himself, *Seven boats. I would love to ride in one of them.*

Then he saw the sign:

Rent a Boat

Good weather (May and June)
$15 per day
Bad weather (all other months)
Free!

Fred smiled and thought, *This is February. It will cost zero dollars to rent a boat.*

Time Out!

I need to explain why the boats are free for most of the year.

In Kansas in May and June, the weather is beautiful. Everyone wants to rent a boat and sail on the lake.

During May and June, a man stays in the boathouse and rents the boats.

During July, August, and September it is too hot and no one wants to rent a boat.

During October, November, December, January, February, March, and April, it is too cold and no one wants to rent a boat.

So during those ten months the man does not stay in the boathouse, and the boats can be used for free.

Fred picked a boat from the left side of the boathouse. Now there were six boats left.

Fred liked boats with sails in the shape of triangles.

Squares are boring. They can just be small or large.

But they can't change shape.

Circles are boring. They can just be small or large.

But circles all look alike.

Triangles are different. They are not boring. They come in all different shapes.

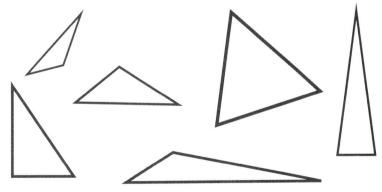

So Fred took a boat with a sail in the shape of a triangle and headed out onto the lake.

There was just a little wind. His boat sailed quietly around on the lake. It was very peaceful.

A bird came, landed on the boat, and looked at Fred.

The bird pointed a wing at the clock on Fred's boat. It was twelve o'clock.

The bird said to Fred, "It is noon. I'm hungry."

Fred got a little nervous. That bird did not look like the birds he was used to seeing around the lake.

Often after a day of teaching, Fred would go out to the lake and feed the ducks.

The bird on Fred's boat did not look like the ducks that Fred liked to feed.

Your Turn to Play

1. When you go out to lunch with a duck, he will have a big salad and lots of bread. Animals that eat plants are called herbivores. (HER-ba-vores)

What Fred was worried about was that the bird on his boat was a carnivore. (CARN-a-vore) Carnivores are animals that eat meat.

Are lions and tigers carnivores?

2. Are kitty cats carnivores?

3. Suppose there are 7 mice and a cat eats 2 of them. How many are left?

4. Suppose there are 7 goldfish and a cat eats 5 of them. How many are left?

5. Suppose there are 7 antelopes and a tiger eats 7 of them. How many are left?

. . . . . . .ANSWERS . . . .

1. Lions and tigers eat meat. They are carnivores.

2. Cats love fish and mice.
Cats are carnivores.

3. $7 - 2 = 5$

4. $7 - 5 = 2$

5. There are zero antelopes left
since $7 - 7 = 0$.

Chapter Eleven
The Hungry Bird

The bird kept looking at Fred. Fred was used to being looked at when he taught math at the college. But this seemed different.

The bird repeated himself, "It is noon, and I am hungry."

Fred said, "I'll be back in a second," and ran downstairs to the kitchen in the boat. He left the bird sitting on the boat.

kitchen

Fred looked around in the kitchen. In one drawer he found a whole bunch of candy.

That's perfect! he thought to himself. *That will fill up that big bird, and he won't be hungry any more.*

Fred put the candy in a large bowl and brought it up. He tried to smile as he offered the bowl to the bird.

"Candy!" the bird shouted. "Who do you think I am? I'm not stupid. That junk will rot my teeth." The bird threw the bowl overboard.

Fred said, "I'll be back in a minute," and ran down to the kitchen again. He found some pancake mix, added some

water, and stirred it. Soon he had a very large stack of pancakes to offer the bird. He wanted the bird to be very full.

Fred put butter on top of the pancakes but didn't add any syrup. He knew the bird didn't like a lot of sugary stuff.

With difficulty he carried the giant plate of pancakes up the stairs and offered it to the bird.

The bird wasn't very interested in the pancakes. He wasn't even looking at them. Instead, he was looking at Fred.

Fred had to ask. "Are you a carni . . . carni . . . carnivore?" He had trouble saying the last word. He was afraid of what the bird was going to answer.

"I'll be back in a minute," Fred said.

Fred raced down the stairs to the kitchen. He opened the refrigerator and found the perfect solution.

Bacon and eggs.

The bird loved them. After he finished eating, he shouted, "More!"

Fred ran downstairs. He cooked five more eggs and five more strips of bacon.

2 eggs + 5 eggs = 7 eggs

2 strips of bacon + 5 strips = 7 strips

The bird was so full that he couldn't fly. He fell off the edge of the boat and had to swim to get to the land.

2 + 5 = 7 had a very happy ending for Fred. He didn't get eaten by the bird.

He looked at the clock on his boat. It was now one o'clock.

Fred took the boat with its sail in the shape of a triangle and headed across the lake. He wanted to get all the way to the other side.

He was so happy that the people who owned the boats had put all that food in the kitchen on the boat. When he got back to the beach house, he was going to leave some money there to pay for the food that he had used.

The sun was shining. The bird was gone. It had turned out to be a beautiful February day.

Fred made up a song and began to sing:

♪♫ The skies are blue in Kansas-land.
Each morning brings its new delights. ♫♪
I thank the One who made all this:
The breeze, the waves, the math I teach,
And students whom I love, their smiles
♫ They offer me. Let's not forget
Those seven eggs and seven strips ♪
Of bacon . . .

Fred stopped singing. Something was happening.

The boat had sprung a leak.

Your Turn to Play

1. Name a set that has seven members.

2. $4 + 3 = ?$

3. $7 + 0 = ?$

4. Counting by fives, write down the numbers from 0 to 20.

5. What is the fourth day of the week?

6. Cows eat grass and other plants.

before lunch   after lunch

Which is true?

   A) Cows are carnivores.

   B) Cows are herbivores.

   C) Cows are crazy.

. . . . ANSWERS . . . .

1. Your answer may be different than mine. I thought of the set of the seven days of the week. The set of the seven eggs. The set of the seven strips of bacon. The set {1, 2, 3, 4, 5, 6, 7}. The set of the seven dwarfs in *Snow White.* The colors of a rainbow {red, orange, yellow, green, blue, indigo, violet}.

2. $4 + 3 = 7$

3. $7 + 0 = 7$ When you add zero to any number, it doesn't change the number.

For example,

   $472,925,503,282,986 + 0 = 472,925,503,282,986$

4. 0, 5, 10, 15, 20

5. Sunday

   Monday

   Tuesday

   Wednesday ☜ the fourth day of the week

6. The correct answer is B) Cows are herbivores.

Chapter Twelve
A Leak

Water was shooting up into the air from the leak. Fred didn't know what to do. He had never been on a boat that was leaking. He tried sitting on the leak. That didn't work. He was too light.

He ran down the stairs to the kitchen. Then he ran down another flight of stairs to the game room that had

a bowling alley,   a chess set,   and a pool table.

He stopped to look at the chess game.
The white king was in trouble.

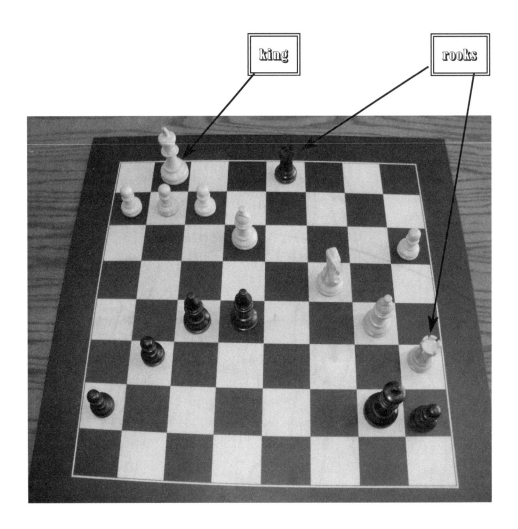

There are six different chess pieces. Once
you learn how each piece moves, you can start to
play. The rooks, for example, can move
vertically ↕ or horizontally ↔.

You now know one-sixth ($\frac{1}{6}$) of all the
chess moves.

But there was no time to waste. He headed down another flight of stairs to the library.

Right there on the fourth shelf from the top was a whole section on boating.

 ← Boating

He looked through the boating titles:

Boats with Bowling Alleys
Bathtub Boats
Kansas Ocean Liners

Fred couldn't believe there was a book on Kansas Ocean Liners. He took it off the shelf and opened it. The pages were blank.

He continued looking.

How to Spell Yacht (not Yought)
Boat Talk: Your Stern Is in the Back
Fixing a Boat Leak

When Fred saw the last title, he shouted,
"Perfect!" and pulled it off the shelf.

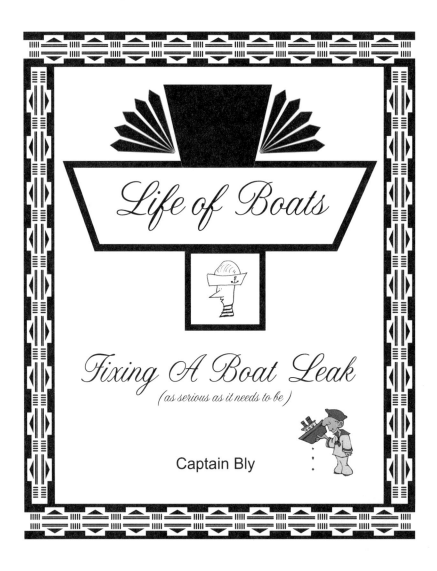

Fred turned to the Table of Contents, which was in the front of the book.

Table of Contents

He took the book over to one of the sofas, sat down, and began to read. He knew he didn't have a very small leak, so he skipped Chapter 1.

When Fred saw the picture of the Titanic, he couldn't resist turning to Chapter 3.

R.M.S. Titanic

The Story of the Titanic

In 1912 the Titanic was the largest passenger ship in the world. It was her first trip (her "maiden voyage").

She was heading from England to New York City. (Ships are often called *she* rather than *it.*)

Titanic was a ship that had almost everything. It had a swimming pool, a gym, libraries, and barber shops.

The best rooms had expensive furniture and fancy wood panels.

There were four electric elevators. In 1912, the use of electricity was very new.

The most expensive ticket for the one-way trip was over $95,000 (in today's dollars).

Titanic was considered a very safe ship. It was divided into large areas called compartments. If a leak developed in a compartment, the watertight doors could be shut. Even if four compartments were flooded, she could stay afloat.

She hit an iceberg, which damaged the ship over a length of 299 feet. (A football field is 300 feet long.) Five compartments were flooded.

Five is greater than four. She sank.

Fred wondered how many watertight compartments there were on his boat.

He ran up the stairs from the library,
passing the game room floor,
passing the kitchen floor, and
up to the top of his boat.

He noticed two things. First, he saw that the leak had stopped. Second, he noticed that the boat had run aground.

Your Turn to Play

1. Fred looked at the two trees. The one on the right was deciduous. Its leaves fall off every winter. The one on the left was an evergreen. Are Christmas trees deciduous or evergreen?

2. What time is it now?

3. 2 + 5 = ?

4. 7 − 1 = ?

5. What is the fifth day of the week?

6. Name a set with ten members in it.

........**ANSWERS**........

1. It would look really weird to have a deciduous Christmas tree. Christmas trees are evergreen.
2. It is two o'clock. This could also be written as 2:00.
3. $2 + 5 = 7$
4. $7 - 1 = 6$
5. Sunday

    Monday

    Tuesday

    Wednesday

    Thursday ☜ the fifth day of the week
6. There are several possible answers. The first set I thought of was {1, 2, 3, 4, 5, 6, 7, 8, 9, 10}.

    Then I thought of the Ten Commandments.

    Then I thought of my ten fingers.

    And my ten toes.

    And the ears that my five best friends have.

Last year after Christmas, a friend of mine took his Christmas tree and put it in his garage. In February, the tree turned brown and looked like this:

The Christmas tree wasn't deciduous. It was dead.

Chapter Thirteen
Silly Duck

Fred hopped off the boat. It was good to be on land again. He pulled the boat on to the shore and put a sign on the side of the boat.

> Warning.
> This boat leaks.

He didn't want anyone to use the boat before the leak was fixed.

On shore, Fred saw three things: an evergreen tree, a deciduous tree, and a duck. There was nothing strange about the trees, but the duck looked a little unusual.

How many unusual things can you see about this duck?

A) He has sunglasses.

B) He is wearing a tie and coat.

C) He is taller than Fred.

Fred is three feet tall. The duck must have been around four feet tall. Most ducks are not four feet tall.

The other thing that was strange about the duck was that he talked. He didn't say, "Quack" like most ducks do.

Instead, he said, "Good morning."

Fred didn't know what to say. It was two in the afternoon.

The duck pointed to the evergreen tree and said, "This tree is deciduous."

Fred didn't know what to think. This was February in Kansas. That tree had all its leaves. It was not deciduous.

Then the duck said, "Three apples plus four apples are 15 apples."

$$3 + 4 \overset{?}{=} 15$$

This is silly, Fred thought to himself. Everyone knows that three apples plus four apples are seven apples.

$$3 + 4 = 7$$

And everyone knows that three plus four does not equal 15.

$$3 + 4 \neq 15$$

Fred might have been wrong about whether it was morning or afternoon.

He might have been wrong about whether that tree was deciduous.

But as a math teacher at KITTENS University, he knew that $3 + 4 \neq 15$.

The duck looked at Fred and said, "You are a bowl of soup."

Fred tried to imagine all the ways that he might be a bowl of soup.

He decided that:

Fred $\neq$ a bowl of soup.

Intermission
for my adult readers only

I am going to put this in tiny type so that kids won't read it. Of course, adults over the age of 40 or 50 typically get presbyopia (reduced ability to focus caused by loss of elasticity of the lenses in eyes because of aging), and they may also have trouble reading this.

The duck has made a lot of false statements. That should not bother us much. We have met people like that. They are either deranged or politicians.

Now suppose the duck said, **I am lying to you Right now.** Is that statement true or false?

If it is true, (**I am lying to you Right now.**), then it must be false.

If it is false, (**I am lying to you Right now.**), then it must be true.

Fred liked the "does not equal" sign. Most things are not equal. If you add two plus five:

$2 + 5 \neq 0$	$2 + 5 \neq 15$	$2 + 5 \neq 30$	$2 + 5 \neq 45$
$2 + 5 \neq 1$	$2 + 5 \neq 16$	$2 + 5 \neq 31$	$2 + 5 \neq 46$
$2 + 5 \neq 2$	$2 + 5 \neq 17$	$2 + 5 \neq 32$	$2 + 5 \neq 47$
$2 + 5 \neq 3$	$2 + 5 \neq 18$	$2 + 5 \neq 33$	$2 + 5 \neq 48$
$2 + 5 \neq 4$	$2 + 5 \neq 19$	$2 + 5 \neq 34$	$2 + 5 \neq 49$
$2 + 5 \neq 5$	$2 + 5 \neq 20$	$2 + 5 \neq 35$	$2 + 5 \neq 50$
$2 + 5 \neq 6$	$2 + 5 \neq 21$	$2 + 5 \neq 36$	$2 + 5 \neq 51$
$2 + 5 = 7$	$2 + 5 \neq 22$	$2 + 5 \neq 37$	$2 + 5 \neq 52$
$2 + 5 \neq 8$	$2 + 5 \neq 23$	$2 + 5 \neq 38$	$2 + 5 \neq 53$
$2 + 5 \neq 9$	$2 + 5 \neq 24$	$2 + 5 \neq 39$	$2 + 5 \neq 54$
$2 + 5 \neq 10$	$2 + 5 \neq 25$	$2 + 5 \neq 40$	$2 + 5 \neq 55$
$2 + 5 \neq 11$	$2 + 5 \neq 26$	$2 + 5 \neq 41$	$2 + 5 \neq 56$
$2 + 5 \neq 12$	$2 + 5 \neq 27$	$2 + 5 \neq 42$	$2 + 5 \neq 57$
$2 + 5 \neq 13$	$2 + 5 \neq 28$	$2 + 5 \neq 43$	$2 + 5 \neq 58$
$2 + 5 \neq 14$	$2 + 5 \neq 29$	$2 + 5 \neq 44$	$2 + 5 \neq 59$

Fred didn't want to be around someone who didn't tell the truth. It was worse than being in a snowstorm without a hat. In both cases your head may start to hurt.

Fred said, "Goodbye," and started jogging.

The last words he heard from the duck were, "I like carrots cooked in gasoline."

Your Turn to Play

1. After being around that duck, it starts to get hard to tell what is true and what is false.

Which of these are true?

$1 + 6 = 7$ $4 + 3 \neq 88$ $555 + 0 = 555$

2. In books for younger readers, you can find problems like $\square + 4 = 7$.

In algebra, they ask the same question by writing $x + 4 = 7$. What does x equal?

3. Name a set that has 12 members in it.

........**ANSWERS**........

1. They are all true.

2. In the books for younger readers, they would write in the book 🔲+ 4 = 7. Of course, this book is different. You do not write in this book.

In algebra you would solve x + 4 = 7, by saying that x = 3.

3. Your answer may be different than mine. I thought of the set of months of the year {January, February, March, April, May, June, July, August, September, October, November, December}.

Or the twelve days of Christmas.

Or {1, 2, 3, 4, 5, 6, 7, 8, 9, 10, 11, 12}.

Or the twelve apostles.

Or the first 12 letters of the Greek alphabet {alpha α, beta β, gamma γ, delta δ, epsilon ε, zeta ζ, eta η, theta θ, iota ι, kappa κ, lambda λ, mu μ,}.

Or the last 12 letters of the Greek alphabet {nu ν, xi ξ, omicron o, pi π, rho ρ, sigma σ, tau τ, upsilon υ, phi φ, chi χ, psi ψ, omega ω}.

Our alphabet {a, b, c, d, . . . } has 26 letters. The Greek alphabet {α, β, γ, δ, . . . } has 24 letters.

Chapter Fourteen
To the Great Woods

Fred was jogging to get away from the duck that didn't tell the truth. In a math book, that duck's lying might be written as:

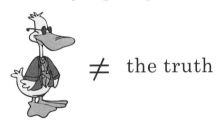 $\neq$ the truth

Fred left the boat and started running around the lake. Fred liked running. It felt good. Sometimes he would hold his arms out like an airplane. Sometimes he would think about what sets he would present in his math classes tomorrow.

☞A set with zero members: {My pet lizards}.

☞A set with one member: {the sun}.

☞A set with two members: {night, day}.

☞A set with three members: {breakfast, lunch, dinner.}

☞A set with four members: {north, east, south, west}.

He thought about drawing triangles inside of circles. That was easy.

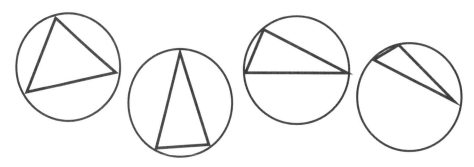

Then he thought of something much harder. Start with a triangle. Can you always draw a circle inside of it?

If you start with a triangle whose sides are equal, it is easy.

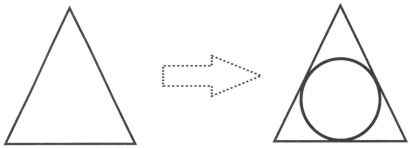

But what about drawing circles inside of other triangles?

Do not write in this book!

Years from now, after you study arithmetic, beginning algebra, and advanced algebra, you will get to geometry. In geometry you will learn the secret of drawing circles inside of any triangle.

Intermission
for my adult readers only

I am going to put this in tiny type so that kids won't read it.

Some kids will be dying to know how to draw a circle inside of any old triangle. Since I'm not telling them how to do it, they may ask you. I'll pass the secret on to you, so that you can appear really smart.

Start with some triangle.

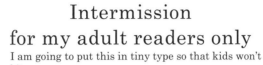

Bisect (cut in half) each angle.

Where the bisectors meet will be the center of the circle.

Fred headed around the lake. He was heading toward the Great Woods.

⇦ The Great Woods

He jogged and jogged. It was three o'clock when he came to the entrance to the Great Woods.

Fred slowed to a walk as he entered the woods. There is a pretty path that goes through the woods. He

could see butterflies playing. They didn't make any noise as they flew.

$\neq$ noise

It was quiet. Fred could think about circles and triangles as he walked through the woods. He could think about big numbers such as one thousand (1,000), and he could think about really small numbers such as zero (0).

Fred liked to count. He started to count up to a thousand—1, 2, 3, 4, 5, 6, . . .—but soon realized that it would take too long.

He started again. This time he was
counting by fives—5, 10, 15, 20, 25, . . .—but
even counting by fives would take too long.

Fred thought of something new. He would
count by hundreds:

one hundred,	100
two hundred,	200
three hundred,	300
four hundred,	400
five hundred,	500
six hundred,	600
seven hundred,	700
eight hundred,	800
nine hundred,	900
one thousand.	1,000

Your Turn to Play

1. Six and one add to seven. $6 + 1 = 7$
Name other pairs of numbers that add to seven.

2. Butterflies don't make a lot of noise. Can you think
of other animals that don't make a lot of noise?

3. On your paper, draw a long skinny triangle like
this:

Can you draw a circle inside of it that touches all three
sides?

·······ANSWERS·······

1. Five and two equals seven. $5 + 2 = 7$

    Two plus five equals seven. $2 + 5 = 7$

    Three plus four equals seven. $3 + 4 = 7$

    Four plus three equals seven. $4 + 3 = 7$

    Seven plus zero equals seven. $7 + 0 = 7$

    Zero plus seven equals seven. $0 + 7 = 7$

2. Your answer may be different than mine.

I did not choose dogs, because they bark.

I did not choose cats, because they meow.

I did not choose ducks, because they quack.

I did not choose cows, because they moo.

    The quietest animal I could think of is a worm.

Actually, this is not a very good drawing of a worm.
Worms do not have noses and eyes.

3. ·

Quack!   silly worm

Chapter Fifteen
In the Great Woods

Fred walked down the path in the Great Woods. He enjoyed the quiet. Since it was February in Kansas, the flowers had not yet started to bloom. Four months from now it would be June, and the Great Woods would be filled with flowers.

The trees in this part of the woods had all their leaves. They were evergreens.

Fred has seen *The Wizard of Oz* movie. In the movie, Dorothy and her friends were in a dark forest, and they were afraid of "lions and tigers and bears."

Fred thought to himself: *But that was just a movie. This is real life. There are no lions or tigers or bears running around in the woods near the KITTENS University campus.*

Intermission
for my adult readers only

I am going to put this in tiny type so that kids won't read it. This literary device is called adumbration (AD-um-BRAY-shun). A faint foreshadowing of what is to come. In Latin, *umbra* means shadow.

Fred headed through the fields. He crossed a little brook. He climbed up a little hill and stood at the very top.

There was a wonderful view. He raised his arms and was about to start singing. Then he noticed something.

He decided to be very quiet. He hoped the lion would not notice that he was standing on its head.

He waited five minutes.

It was now five minutes after three o'clock. 3:05

The lion didn't move. Fred didn't move. A butterfly landed on Fred's head, and then it flew away.

It was now ten minutes after three. 3:10

     The lion didn't move. Fred didn't move.

It was now fifteen minutes after three. 3:15

     Nobody moved.

3:20

3:25

Can you see why people learn to count by fives?

Fred needed to do something. He carefully looked down at the lion. It was not moving at all. It didn't even blink.

The lion's hair felt very hard. He waited another five minutes just to make sure.

   3:30

Then he hopped off of the lion. The lion didn't move. It was a statue. There was a sign near the lion:

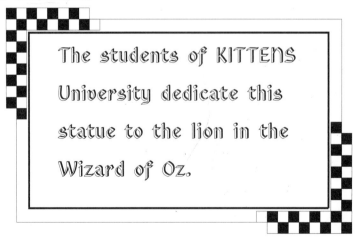

The students of KITTENS University dedicate this statue to the lion in the Wizard of Oz.

Your Turn to Play

1. 4 + 3 = ?
2. 7 − 3 = ?
3. What time is it?

. . . . **ANSWERS** . . . .

1. $4 + 3 = 7$
2. $7 - 3 = 4$

 Six o'clock   6:00

 Fifteen minutes
after six o'clock   6:15

 Ten minutes
after four o'clock   4:10

Chapter Sixteen
Embarrassed

Fred felt a little embarrassed. He had been fooled by a statue. He hoped that no one had seen him standing on that statue of the lion for 30 minutes (from 3:00 to 3:30).

Then he turned and saw this girl who had been watching him.

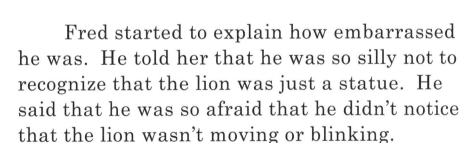

Fred started to explain how embarrassed he was. He told her that he was so silly not to recognize that the lion was just a statue. He said that he was so afraid that he didn't notice that the lion wasn't moving or blinking.

He said to her, "I bet you were not afraid, since you are so much bigger than I am."

She didn't blink.

The students of KITTENS University dedicate this statue to Dorothy in the Wizard of Oz.

The first part of *The Wizard of Oz* takes place in Kansas, which is where Fred lives. The students at the university love the story and built these statues in the Great Woods.

He found the statue of the Scarecrow. He walked up to the statue and felt the straw.

He walked up to the statue of Dorothy's dog and gave him a pat on the head.

He wasn't even afraid of the statue of the winged monkey. He walked up to it and . . . the monkey ran away!

It was one of the monkeys who lived in the Great Woods.

"Wait!" Fred shouted. "I won't hurt you."

The monkey came back with his six friends.

Fred asked one of the monkeys, "What do you do all day long? I know you don't stand still like the statues."

 The monkey said, "We just monkey around.

✓ We can't read, so we don't get smart.

✓ We don't work, so we don't make money.

✓ We just watch a lot of television."

Fred took a tennis ball out of his pocket and rolled it toward one of the monkeys.

Four of the monkeys made a rectangle and started playing catch with the ball.

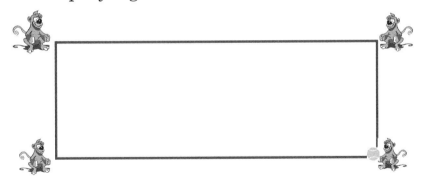

There were seven monkeys. Four of them were standing at the corners of a rectangle playing catch with Fred's ball. The other three monkeys couldn't make a rectangle.

So they made a triangle. Since they didn't have a ball to play with, they used Fred.

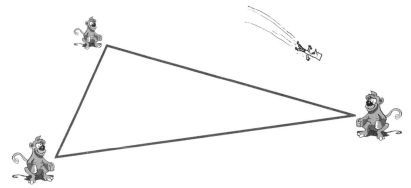

At first, Fred was frightened, but after a while it became fun. He was happy they were playing catch and not football with him!

After a while, the monkeys got tired and went back to watching television.

4:00

Fred didn't want to spend his time watching some clown on television. It was getting late and he needed to get home to take care of his doll, Kingie.

Your Turn to Play

1. On a piece of paper, draw a rectangle where all four sides have the same length. What do you call this special rectangle?

2. Draw a figure that has four sides that is not a rectangle.

3. Draw a figure that has five sides.

4. How many sides does a stop sign have?

5. 5 + 2 = ?

6. If tomorrow is Tuesday, what day is today?

7. If an hour from now it will be five o'clock, what time is it now?

8. If a month from now it will be March, what month is it now?

......ANSWERS.......

1. If you take a rectangle and make all four sides equal, you get a square.

2. There are lots of four-sided figures that are not rectangles.

3. You could make all five sides have the same length, or you could make all five sides have different lengths.

 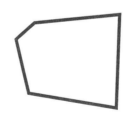

4. Stop signs have eight sides.

5. $5 + 2 = 7$

6. The day before Tuesday is Monday.

7. The hour before five o'clock is four o'clock.

8. The month before March is February.

Chapter Seventeen
Going Home

Fred ran up the two flights of stairs to his office. He walked past the vending machines in the hallway toward his office. There was a new sign on his office door.

Kingie's
Art
Studio

Fred slowly opened the door. He didn't know what to expect. The room smelled like oil paint.

Kingie had changed clothes. He was painting a picture.

Kingie said, "I got tired of just doing drawings, so I have switched to doing oil paintings."

Fred rubbed his eyes. He couldn't believe what Kingie had done. The walls were filled with oil paintings.

Kingie said, "I am just learning. After I have practiced for a couple more years, I will get better."

Fred had been drawing for five years. Here was Fred's picture of a house and trees that he drew yesterday.

Fred asked, "You did all these paintings today?"

"No," Kingie answered. "This morning I read three books from your library on how to do oil painting. Then I had lunch. I did these six paintings this afternoon. I'm working on my seventh painting right now."

Fred looked over Kingie's shoulder.

Fred was silent. He wondered if Heaven would look like that.

Fred looked at the clock. It was 4:35.

He headed over to his desk. He wanted to get ready for teaching tomorrow's classes.

His notes for his arithmetic class:

> arithmetic
>
> The number zero.
> It makes 100 a lot
> bigger than 1.
>
> Zero is the largest
> number of whales I
> can fit in my pocket.
> $0 + 527 = 527$

His notes for his algebra and geometry classes:

> algebra
>
> Algebra is the game
> of trying to figure
> out what x could
> equal when it hides
> in an equation.
>   What is x in
> $x + 4 = 7$?
>   answer: $x = 3$

> geometry
>
> Rectangles have 4
> sides and square
> corners.
>
> These are not
> rectangles:
>
> Corners not   Too many
> square   sides

Your Turn to Play

1. Fred did many silly things when he was teaching. In his arithmetic class, he once brought in three football helmets.

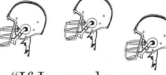

He asked his class, "If I were hungry, how many football helmets could I eat?"

What is the correct answer?

2. What time is it?

3. What is the third day of the week?

4. If tomorrow will be Tuesday, what day of the week was yesterday?

5. Find the value of x that makes this true:

$$x + 1 = 7$$

. . . . ANSWERS . . . .

1. Even if he were really hungry, he couldn't eat any football helmets. The correct answer is zero helmets.

2. It is twenty minutes
after 3 o'clock.   3:20

3. Sunday

    Monday

    Tuesday   ☞ the third day of the week

4. If tomorrow will be Tuesday, then today must be Monday.

    If today is Monday, then yesterday must have been Sunday.

5. $x + 1 = 7$ when $x = 6$.

Chapter Eighteen
Vending Machines

When Fred had finished writing his notes for tomorrow's classes and Kingie had finished painting his seventh picture, they looked at each other.

It was quiet for a moment.

Then Fred spoke. "There were no classes today because of the bad weather. I hope there are classes tomorrow."

Just then they heard a *ker-flop* as the evening newspaper was delivered. Fred hopped off of his chair and opened the door.

He looked down the hallway where the vending machines were.

In front of the hot roast beef sandwich machine was the hungry bird. It put a dime into the machine.

The machine made a little noise and out popped a hot roast beef sandwich.

Because he was a carnivore, he threw away the bread and just ate the meat.

A dime is worth ten cents. 10¢

Things are often a lot cheaper at KITTENS University. At most places you cannot buy a hot roast beef sandwich for a dime.

One dime = 10¢ = 1¢ + 1¢ + 1¢ + 1¢ + 1¢ +
                  1¢ + 1¢ + 1¢ + 1¢ + 1¢.

Or, counting by fives: 5, 10.

10¢ = 5¢ + 5¢.

In front of another vending machine was the duck that couldn't tell the truth. The duck was standing in front of the soft drink machine and said:

Fred picked up the newspaper and headed back into his office. He shut the door leaving the hungry bird and the duck outside.

Fred opened the evening newspaper and gave the comics section to Kingie. Since the KITTEN Caboodle newspaper was very small, it had only one comic strip. Kingie always giggled when he read it.

Today was different. When Kingie looked at the comic strip, he did not giggle. He cried.

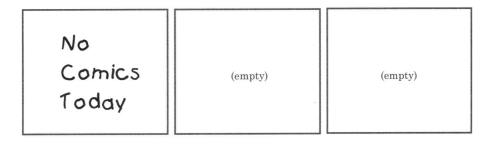

Fred turned to the front paper of the newspaper.

THE KITTEN Caboodle

The Official Campus Newspaper of KITTENS University Monday evening   10¢

No Comic Strip Today!

KANSAS: All of the campus was sad today. The man who drew our comic strip retired today. He had been drawing his comic strip in this paper since the university began back in 1929.

A party was held in his honor this afternoon. All the students came to the party. Almost all the teachers came. The only teacher that didn't come was Fred

Fred missed the party

Gauss. When someone came to his office to tell Fred about the party, no one was there except his doll. His doll didn't know where Fred was.

page 2

Contest Announced

We need a new person to draw the comic strip for our newspaper.

All students and teachers can enter the contest. Send in your strip.

The person who draws the funniest strip will win.

advertisement

NEW COAT!

Wear it
    in the snow!
Wear it
    in the rain!

If it gets too hot, you can take it off!

Fred and Kingie looked at each other. They knew what they wanted to do. They would enter the contest.

Fred ran to his desk and pulled out a piece of paper.

Kingie squeezed out some more oil paint. He told Fred that he would be the first comic strip artist to use oil paints.

Fred looked at the blank sheet of paper. He didn't know where to begin. He had never drawn a comic strip before. He had a lot of questions:

How big do I make it?

Do I use pencil or pen?

Can I use crayons?

Fred knew where to find the answers to his questions. Most of the walls in his office were covered with books. He went and found books on drawing comic strips.

One book gave a list of the things he would need to begin. Another book told Fred about drawing shadows. A third book showed how to start drawing faces. The book gave some examples:

Then Fred tried:

Your Turn to Play

1. Kingie looked at Fred's book. Here is the drawing that Kingie made.

Kingie looked at the clock. What time is it?

2. 5 + 2 = ?

3. Fred drew a comic strip of a dog eating the number eight. He thought that was funny. Be an artist and draw your own funny comic strip.

4. How many members does this set have {1, 2, 3, 4, 5, 6, 7, 8} ?

·······ANSWERS·······

1.  It is five o'clock. 5:00

2. 5+ 2 = 7

3. Here is the strip that Fred drew:

4. {1, 2, 3, 4, 5, 6, 7, 8} has eight members.

It had been a long day. Lots of things had happened. They were tired of drawing. Kingie and Fred put away all their art supplies.

Kingie asked Fred to read a story to him.

Fred picked out a book about butterflies. He went and sat in the corner of his room and put Kingie on his lap.

When Fred was about half way through the book, Kingie shut his eyes and fell asleep. Kingie was dreaming about butterflies.

Index

If you would like to
learn more about
books written about
Fred . . .

FredGauss.com

Gauss is Fred's last name.

It rhymes with house.